51 Things
You Should Know Before
Getting Engaged

51 Things
You Should Know Before
Getting Engaged

Michael Batshaw

TRADE PAPER
PRESS

Turner Publishing Company
200 4th Avenue North • Suite 950
Nashville, Tennessee 37219
(615) 255-2665

www.turnerpublishing.com

51 Things You Should Know Before Getting Engaged

Copyright © 2009 Trade Paper Press

Library of Congress Cataloging-in-Publication Data

Batshaw, Michael.
51 things you should know before getting engaged / Michael Batshaw.
    p. cm.
Includes bibliographical references.
ISBN 978-1-59652-548-1
1. Courtship. 2. Marriage. 3. Betrothal. I. Title. II. Title: Fifty-one things you should know before getting engaged.
HQ801.B3437 2009
306.73'4--dc22

                          2009016351

Printed in China

09 10 11 12 13 14 15 16—0 9 8 7 6 5 4 3 2 1

For my wife, Natasha.
Thank you for everything!

You come to love not by finding the perfect person,
but by seeing an imperfect person perfectly.

~ Sam Keen

Love seems the swiftest, but it is the slowest of all growths.
No man or woman really knows what perfect love is until
they have been married a quarter of a century.

~ Mark Twain

Contents

Introduction

Introduction

The decision to get engaged is one of the most exciting and important ones you will ever make in your life. As a husband and a father, I have seen firsthand the profound effects of this choice. As a psychotherapist, I see individuals and couples at each stage of the journey, both before and long after this decision has been made. I wrote this book to address some of the most common questions I see people wrestle with before engagement:

- Is the person I'm dating the person I want to marry?
- People change so much; what if I make the wrong choice?
- Things are really good now, but how do I know that we won't grow apart?
- How do I know he won't be more attracted to

somebody else in the future?
- How do I know that I'll still love her years later?

Here are some complaints I hear from people who are already married:

- I should have gotten to know him better. I rushed in because we were so in love.
- I didn't know how to tell whether he was really the best partner in the long run.
- It was so good at the beginning, and then things just fell apart.
- We never really got to know each other well.
- We were just going along with the flow, and I didn't know it would be this hard and this complicated to live with somebody.
- I knew he had these issues, but I wish I had taken it more seriously.
- I wish I had known myself better.

Although therapy can help some of these couples, clearly they could have benefited from some guidance before they got engaged. Sadly, many of these marriages may end up in long-term unhappiness or divorce.

Statistics have long put the divorce rate in this country at roughly 50 percent of all marriages. Why is this? I believe that many people are not properly prepared for the complexities that come with committed adult relationships. There are two key areas where there is a lack of guidance: (1) Having the self-awareness and proper perspective to make the right choice in a partner; (2) Having the tools and techniques necessary to navigate the inevitable trials of a long-term relationship.

The path to engagement is much like any other adventure in life—travel, career, buying a house—all of them pleasures and challenges we pursue best with care and forethought. I have often wondered why people in general don't put the same care and forethought into engagement and marriage as they do into these other endeavors.

Let's say, for example, you are very excited about going trekking in the Himalayas. You would be facing the possibility of transformative, exciting new experiences, with the potential to change yourself and the way you look at the world. In life's adventures, both the path and the place always have the power to change and expand you. But if you strap on your backpack and just set off, hasty, naive, unprepared, and uninformed, then the adventure has the ability to crush you, destroy your confidence, and send you home defeated. I have seen many individuals at different stages of a relationship that looked just this way.

Few would go under-informed and over-emotional into the snow and mountains of the Himalayas. Anyone attempting the path of sub-zero temperatures, sudden blizzards, and icy glaciers, without intense research about the terrain, without the necessary experience, and without a good guide and guidebook would be destined for certain doom. These preparations allow the adventurer to understand clearly what he or she is getting into, what the risks are, what tools to bring, what skills need to be developed, and how to evaluate his or her team for success in the journey. Furthermore, this knowledge permits adjustments while on the path, reducing the chances of having to simply pack it up and be resigned to failure.

Why don't we approach engagement with this degree of preparation and guidance? I believe much of the fault lies in how our popular culture portrays love and marriage. Society encourages us to dive in without looking back when we feel intensely about someone. The idea is, "Rush forward, trust your emotions completely, and keep that good feeling going. If you feel that strong desire for someone and you can keep that feeling going long enough, it may be true love, which of course conquers all."

Now, if you were visiting Nepal and you fell in love with the mountains, felt an incredible passion and pull to climb them, what would you do? It is unlikely that anyone would advise you to "trust your feelings, take off, make haste, follow your passion, and the rest will take care of itself." Anyone following such advice would freeze to death in one day. The moral of the story is that people tend to be much more cautious when their lack of knowledge and skill leads to probable death! But in the case of making the choice to get engaged, the possibility of crippling unhappiness, disappointment, and disillusionment in marriage seems inconceivable to a young couple in love.

How the 51 Things Can Help

In this book, I provide the perspective and the tools necessary to have a successful engagement and marriage.

Getting engaged and then getting married carries with it the possibility to transform you in untold, wonderful ways. You can grow into the person and the couple you always dreamed of, and surprise yourself and each other again and again.

Every adventurer needs a guidebook. My goal in writing this book is to create a handy, back-pocket, personal Sherpa to lead you into your engagement and beyond. When you are on a trek and reach an obstacle, and you are not exactly sure what to do, you don't want to reach for the complete, exhaustive history of Himalayan trekking over the last two thousand years. You want to be able to open to a page that has a map of the terrain, showing you the way to proceed around that particular obstacle in simple, easy-to-follow steps.

Most of us, pressed for time in a busy world, think about our relationship on the way to work, during lunch break, or at night before we go to bed. This book, *51 Things You Should Know Before Getting Engaged,* is the simplest map for busy Americans to insights and techniques for greater clarity in deciding if your partner is the right one for you, and if that person is the right one, how to keep it that way by honing your communication skills and learning how to structure a healthy, vibrant future together.

I have included a single brief question at the end of each of the 51 steps. These questions are meant to stimulate you to think more deeply about how each chapter relates to your unique experience with your mate.

Are you ready to follow these 51 Things to a good relationship? If so, then let's get started.

The 51 Things

~ 1 ~

One hardly ever hears, "I wish I had gotten engaged earlier"

How long should one wait before getting engaged? Of course, there is no gold standard timeline for all relationships to enter into such a commitment. However, there are certainly some milestones that should be passed before the big engagement ensues.

First, don't get engaged before you have become sufficiently annoyed at and resentful of certain aspects of your partner's personality. It's essential to have the visceral experience of such annoyances and resentments in order to heighten your awareness and deepen your understanding regarding your partner's strengths and weaknesses. As a couple, you should have had many arguments and have resolved them well, resulting in greater intimacy. The majority of individuals considering engagement are already having sex. For those individuals, sex should be good and it should be improving in some ways. People who have decided to wait until marriage should have thoroughly discussed their views and feelings about sex with their mate. One should always discuss major value systems and life goals, thereby ensuring that the two of you are essentially compatible.

I do not believe it is absolutely necessary to live with each other before you get engaged. However, by the time you are ready to pop the question, you should be spending most days of the week together. It is very important to know that the daily living habits of your partner are compatible with yours and that you can work toward resolving the ones that conflict. Last, you can feel confident moving forward with your engagement when you see your partner actively involved in working on personal issues which otherwise could present a problem for the relationship.

Many couples have asked me to give them a rough time estimate for engagement. In general, I tell them they'd have to be in a state of denial to miss seeing most of each other's faults after roughly two years of being together. Some couples may come to this point a little earlier; others much later. Still, in my estimation, it's pretty difficult to know if you are truly compatible in less than that span of time. Kindly remember: no matter how well you strive to get to know each other, there is a natural timeline along which relationships evolve. In other words, you can't bake bread in five minutes at two thousand degrees. Certain things just take time, and in this case the time spent goes a long way toward ensuring that your ultimate decision will be based not solely on a feeling of love for your partner, but also on the evidence that you have already taken strides toward building a stable, loving relationship.

Have you been with your partner long enough to grow annoyed at certain aspects of that person's personality?

‐ 2 ‐

Hollywood gets it wrong

The sentence "This isn't how it happens in the movies" has been uttered by many a person after the first nine months or so in a new relationship. Like some stereotypes, Hollywood's portrayal of the bloom of first love, passion, and overcoming odds and adversity has some basis in real life—that's one of the reasons we may relate to certain characters and situations. We imagine, based on our experience perhaps, things really could be this way, so we suspend disbelief and are drawn into the action. And, if we're lucky, maybe for an hour, or a day, or a month or two—they are. But the nuts and bolts of working through the hard stuff in a relationship are rarely fully fleshed out on the silver screen. Hollywood's portrayal of romance has a potent, influential effect on what we feel a relationship should really be with another person, and is capable of diverting our attention from what it actually is. Strange that Hollywood dictates reality for so many, since we ourselves are in fact the real people, and the ones on screen are the fantasies or caricatures of us!

Films and TV shows often contrast the beauty and purity of youthful love, full of promise and passion, with the old, stale, "out of touch" relationships of the characters' elders. This sets up an unfortunate dilemma: we feel we must embody the passionate, optimistic, empathic love of youth and early relationships or else be crushed by the empty, lifeless shell of the boring, pay-the-bills, drive-the-minivan, take-out-the-garbage, workaday reality of our parents. As if these two simplified, polar opposite pictures were the only two options in life! Hollywood would like to sell us on these extreme, opposite caricatures because they make for far better drama on screen.

We can't let ourselves be controlled internally by such black-and-white simplifications of real relationships. You can have a real, intimate partnership while at the same time embracing the responsibilities of adulthood. In other words, like most things in life, there is a *lot* of richly hued gray! As time passes and a relationship between two open people matures, shared passion grows and leaves you more satisfied year by year than the best-written two-hour or even ten-hour-long film could possibly show.

> *Do you find yourself wishing your relationship was more like a fairy tale or Hollywood movie?*

— 3 —

Beware of the person of your dreams

Each of us has outlined in our mind some image of the "dream" partner. This idealized image is likely formed from a blend of conscious needs and unconscious desires. There are aspects of a partner that draw us to that person in full awareness: "I find her very physically attractive . . . He is clearly intelligent . . . I like the way he takes care of me. . . ." All of these are wonderful qualities you should identify in a partner. The other aspect of what attracts us to the dream partner is his role in completing for us some unfinished or unresolved relationship from our past. The partner may resemble a mother, or brother, or a former lover in some strange way. One often asks, "How could I have chosen someone who seemed so different from my father at first and then ended up so much like him years later?"

This is a common occurrence as we are drawn, in what seems to us an inexplicable manner, toward individuals who are familiar to us in some deep way. One tragic example is that of the abused woman. First, her father abuses her, and then she seemingly inexplicably chooses man after man who abuses her. However, with each new man, she swears to both herself and often to those concerned about her that this man is completely different from her father or former boyfriend.

We all have hidden relationship templates. The person whom we feel most strongly drawn to, who gives us the biggest "rush," is not always the best person for us. Usually that person embodies to some degree someone from our past, not necessarily those of the romantic sort. The rush of feeling welling up within us in response to this figure is the siren song that draws us to try to resolve the pain of a past relationship with this new "dream" partner. Unfortunately, once we are side-by-side with this person, we may find someone who causes us to re-experience many of the old, problematic issues we thought we had moved beyond.

So, when the dream partner materializes, step back and consider things for a bit longer. Make sure that you are seeing things clearly. If you are, you will avoid reliving the past over and over again, and start working toward a new future of great possibilities.

Does your mate remind you in any way of someone who has hurt you in the past?

— 4 —

If you put your partner on a pedestal, take him off

First things first: pedestals are for statues, not for people. I admit, it's enjoyable to look up at a statue and admire its sculptured perfection. You might ask yourself, though: Who would that perfect partner be? The most attractive, smart, kind, loving person ever? You might even believe you've found someone who has everything you've ever looked for in a mate and, indeed, your partner probably does have many wonderful attributes.

Like it or not, we are all flawed. We disappoint and we fall short of expectations. At times we are selfish, arrogant, lazy, mistrustful, and sometimes we even lie. The hope is that we keep these behaviors in check most of the time, aware of our imperfections and continually at work toward bettering ourselves. Still, if I had a dollar for every time I've heard someone in my office say, "He wasn't like this in the beginning" or "She isn't who I thought she was" or "How come I didn't see any of this before?" I would be a wealthy man. There's a reason almost all of the great plays and movies about finding romance end in a wedding and not a marriage. We are often so enamored with the initial "honeymoon" part of the relationship that we miss seeing the person as a whole.

Don't get me wrong. I am a big fan of "feeling good," even of "feeling great!" Better yet—"feeling better than I ever have in my entire life!" And yet, we must strive to see our partner clearly. This means not whitewashing or shying away from seeing the human, flawed side of your beloved. To get to this clarity, take him off the pedestal so that you can bring him to eye level. Then you will see that he too is a "wonderfully flawed" person, real and dimensional—just like you.

Do you think your partner is perfect in almost every way?

— 5 —

If you find yourself on a pedestal, get off

Everyone loves to be adored. And why not? Having your beloved desire you, compliment you, rush to meet your every need sounds great. So, what's the problem? Unfortunately, none of us is so perpetually wonderful that we deserve such constant admiration. In the beginning of a relationship, it may be easy to show only your best side.

Inevitably, as intimacy grows, we get hurt in some way and end up contradicting, to different degrees, this wonderful image our partner has of us—the marble gets chipped. There are two typical reactions to this fall from grace. One, your partner may feel betrayed and tricked by his muse, who is not a goddess after all, but an ordinary person, like himself. Two, he might make excuses and blame himself for your less-than-perfect actions. Either way, this can be a very tricky phase of the relationship. It is always of the utmost importance to remember that you are a special, adorable person in so many ways. However, you are also an imperfect person, and your partner will find that out sooner or later. It isn't a matter of if, it is a matter of when.

It is always best to recognize this dynamic when it arises and nip it in the bud. Do yourself a favor: Step off the pedestal, look into your partner's eyes, and say, "Here I am. I want you to see and accept all of me, the best and the not so pretty." It is in this place of equality and realness that true love can blossom.

> *Does your partner find you perfect and wait on you hand and foot?*

— 6 —

Great sex will not save a mediocre relationship

Good sex is a necessary element of any stable, lively, and fun relationship. Sex is the engine, the motivating force that powers and deepens the intimate connection between two people throughout their lives together. Truth be told, I can't say enough about the positive value of good sex for a healthy relationship. However, good sex is not sufficient, in and of itself, to produce a sustainable long-term connection.

I see many couples on the cusp of divorce who question why they stayed together for ten years when it was so clear to everyone around them how bad the relationship was. Some of them fought all the time and were inherently incompatible in so many ways, although both steadfastly maintain, "Well, we had good sex"—perhaps shocked, and maybe even a little dismayed, that this was not enough. Such observations illustrate a few important things about the relationship between good sex and personal connection. First, good sex enables couples to continue to ignore the degree to which their relationship isn't working when things aren't going well. Such couples may come to use sex like a feel-good drug that temporarily banishes bad feelings, thereby enabling them to ignore, if only for the moment, the painful recognition that they are ultimately incompatible.

Second, if this couple had not had such good sex, they might have given up on the relationship much earlier, sparing both of them a great deal of emotional turmoil and aiding them as individuals to find a more holistically compatible partner. What are we to take away from this cautionary tale? If you keep coming back to "good sex" as the primary reason for your "good" relationship, step back and look more closely. Sexual compatibility does not mean healthy intimacy, mutual respect, or even emotional compatibility. It simply means you have good physical chemistry together, and good physical chemistry is a great thing to have—but it isn't nearly enough to stake your future happiness on.

Is good sex one of the few redeeming qualities of your relationship?

– 7 –

Mediocre sex can become great sex with patience and determination

I find that there are few couples who are truly happy when they have a less than satisfactory sex life. In most cases, a disappointing sex life will lead to other problems in the relationship. Conversely, problems in the relationship will lead to problems in bed. Sex is fundamentally about communication, physical and mental, and is the most explicit act of love two partners can share with one another. Some couples naturally have great sexual chemistry and communication, like two dancers meant to tango with each other. However, even the most compatible partners need time to familiarize themselves with each other's rhythms. Most couples do not automatically know what the other will and won't like, and that's O.K. Fortunately, we can get to know the needs and desires of our mate through communication, experimentation, and practice. That may sound simple enough, an easy prescription anyone should be able to confidently follow.

Still, few are more discouraged about their relationship or its future prospects than those with less-than-satisfactory sex lives. Many ask themselves, "Is this a sign we're incompatible? If he were the right one, wouldn't he know just how to touch me and be with me?" These couples can be plagued with doubt, and that doubt gets reinforced with each unsuccessful venture. This is truly a sad circumstance to encounter as a therapist in that it often amazes me how readily and rapidly a couple's sex life improves when meaningful dialogue about the issue is undertaken between them. Talk to each other. Take your time. If you're both willing to learn about yourselves and each other, in time, with some effort, your sex life will surprise you, and it will become great.

Do you find your sex life with your mate lacking?

— 8 —

You have to know your own flaws, imperfections, and weaknesses. Admit them to yourself and your partner

L et me start by saying that nobody wants to do this, myself included. We are always taught that first impressions are everything: put your best foot forward; people form their impressions of you in the first thirty seconds; learn how to influence people's perceptions of you. These skills make us feel more in control of our interpersonal relationships. We develop these skills in order to help us make friends, get ahead at work, and entice a romantic partner.

Many of us grow up feeling that if we are perfect enough, or good enough, then maybe we can get the things we want in life. However, if we are not good enough, then we can't compete with others and we will end up as failures. Furthermore, we have to compete for the affection of those we are attracted to, and so we strive to show ourselves in the most positive light possible. The tragedy of this position is that we are all flawed and imperfect, whether we like it or not. These imperfections can come out most strongly in intimate relationships in which we tend to let our defenses down over time. It is necessary to be vulnerable in this way in order to build greater intimacy and feel truly loved and cared for by your partner. However, this sets up a conflict with our usual state of being, in which we spend much of our time managing others' perceptions of us to ward off feelings of insecurity, shame, or guilt, which are inevitable at times in life. Most of us have experienced our fair share of these painful feelings in childhood and don't want any part of that now.

Let me be clear: I am not suggesting that, on your first date, you present a list of all your faults and problems and ask the person if she thinks she's up to dealing with all your insecurities. What I am talking about is that when you've been together for enough time that you are considering getting engaged and married, you need to take a look at this issue. If you have not been forthcoming about your imperfections, now is the time to start showing more of them to your partner. The paradox of all this is that the more you reveal your weaknesses and still continue to be accepted and loved by your partner, the more you will feel safer than ever in your relationship.

The experience of being loved deeply, even with your flaws openly exposed, is one of the richest, fullest, and most positive experiences you will ever have in your life. The feeling of security and freedom in the relationship allows you to build a foundation that will enable you to withstand the many great storms that will come, often unexpectedly, in your married life. And, instead of the secret fear that your partner will someday really know that side of you, you'll feel that the more she knows and the more you share, the better your relationship will become.

Are you hiding your weaknesses from your partner?

$-9-$

What is your partner's true character? These qualities are not likely to change much in the future

What defines a person's character? Character is made up of those qualities that have consistently defined a person's beliefs and actions across all domains in her life. Qualities such as being empathic, hardworking, gentle, or funny are a combination of innate temperament, developed value systems, and habits of behavior in life. These qualities tend to remain fairly stable throughout a person's life. For example, a woman does not over time just stop having a sense of humor, lose her sense of empathy, and stop feeling responsible for others. If these qualities do change quickly in a relationship, it is probably because the person was not being entirely genuine in the beginning of the relationship, in an attempt to "keep up appearances."

Character can be defined as the very essence of a person. I cannot overstress how important it is to discern the character of your mate. Does she behave with others as she does with me? Does he respect my friends? Does she value family and friendships? Does he always try to do the right thing, even at risk of personal expense? These are the kinds of questions you should consider. If she frequently contradicts herself and shows questionable character in some circumstances, call her on it and ask her to explain herself.

No one is perfect. The point here is not to seek someone with perfect character, but rather to find someone whose character you respect and who, when she contradicts herself, can recognize it, accept feedback, and acknowledge she does not want to behave in that manner. If your partner is always defensive in such situations, be cautious: she may not have the insight or intent to become a woman of greater character. Remember, character will be with you forever, a constant in the sea of life's unpredictable demands and changing social circumstances—and it absolutely can improve, but only by means of awareness, desire, and hard work.

> *Does your potential spouse act with integrity while interacting at work, with friends, and with family?*

‒ 10 ‒

Get to know your partner's relationship history and patterns

A question that comes up for most people at differing stages in a relationship is, Just how well do I know my partner? You may feel you know your partner very well in some areas and not well in others. You may wonder if you know him well enough to trust him or to feel secure about his commitment to you. These are a few of the unknowns everyone must grapple with when taking the next step in a relationship. However, you are not without certain important precedents that can give you clues as to what to watch for in the future. These important clues are found in the stories of your partner's previous intimate relationships. By getting to know the patterns of your partner's past relationships, you will gain a greater awareness of his behavior and possible challenges for him.

Although some may wish to avoid such topics, having a discussion about these issues is one of the best ways to assess the potential for past patterns to re-emerge and cause conflict in your current relationship. Sometimes, when you have this discussion, your significant other will paint the picture that there was a general incompatibility that caused a past relationship (or several) to fail, and it is certainly possible this is accurate. However, such a picture doesn't answer the question why. Why was your partner with this wholly incompatible person, perhaps for a long while, in the first place? Why did he stay involved as long as he did? What were the specific reasons the relationship ended?

I'm not suggesting you break out the bright lights and brush up on your interrogation techniques prior to having such a discussion. Rather, I am suggesting a dialogue built upon genuine curiosity. Increasing your awareness of your own relationship issues and those of your partner's makes you vastly more informed when it comes time to deal with the inevitable struggles each relationship brings. Remember, in this landscape of intimacy, knowledge of the territory is power, and the more you understand his past paths through this terrain, the greater chance you both have of avoiding similar mistakes and building upon past successes for the betterment of your own walk together.

> *Do you know most of the important details about your partner's past relationships?*

— 11 —

Look carefully at how your partner takes care of himself

Youth allows us many indulgences, and those pleasures are rarely destructive. We can stay out all night, drink till we stumble, eat whatever pleases us, never visit a doctor, and, knock on wood, survive young adulthood with little apparent detriment. I challenge you to look underneath your partner's external appearance. He may look fit, have a good job, and have friends. In fact, everything may be checked off on your lengthy list of things to look for in a man. But observe: Does he ever exercise? Does he attend to daily stress? When there's a problem at work or with family or friends, does he ignore it, dismiss it, or face it head-on even if it is incredibly challenging? People can only care for themselves if they really look at themselves.

Pay careful attention: your partner's looks and good

fortune are a gift of youth. Partners will only age well in all respects if they are taking the messages their body and mind are giving them and responding attentively to address these issues. In terms of maintaining a healthy body and mind, it is critical that both you and your partner are moving in the same direction. Remember, taking care of another person begins with taking care of yourself.

Do you have concerns about the way your partner takes care of himself?

~ 12 ~

Daily living habits may be more important than you realize

We can't hide the way we live when someone either lives with us or spends a large amount of time in our home. So, whether you actually live together or just spend most nights together, you will get ample exposure to your partner's domestic habits. Although couples tend to be on their best behavior in the beginning, once you feel more secure, your true colors will shine through. Does he put the dishes away or leave them in the sink for days? Does she put the cap back on the toothpaste? Does he regularly stock his refrigerator with food? Does her place have the look and feel of an adult's or that of a college student? Once these living habits become apparent, you'll want to assess which ones are and are not compatible with your own way of living. If you find most of his domestic style unacceptable, you may have a real problem on your hands.

People's habits of daily living are deeply ingrained, and although they can change quite a bit over time, it takes patience and motivation. Talking about this subject can be touchy, so remember to be very respectful and empathetic. Always seek to understand why he might live the way he does before you decide to judge him. It is always best to enter into a difficult conversation from the standpoint of love and understanding. Your potential spouse does not have to be just like you in every way. Still, if you are thinking of creating a home together and building a future, you will both need to make acceptable compromises that you can live with over time.

Finally, don't wait long to resolve this issue. Don't minimize its importance because other things are so good. If you have incompatible living styles, you may experience growing resentment over time. Be honest, empathetic, and up front about your desire to discuss these issues before you make the jump to create a home and a life together.

> *Are your daily domestic habits compatible with those of your mate?*

~ 13 ~

You must respect what your partner does for a living

Many times I've heard someone say with sadness in her voice, "I really like him, he is a really good person, but I don't respect what he does for a living and I'm afraid I never will." The conflict this woman is presenting is a common one among many couples. What to do? How do I proceed if I don't really respect my partner's job?

The first thing you must do is understand what it means to not respect his job. Let's say your fiancé works in business; he has not progressed in his field over many years, but he keeps plugging away, and you know he has no history of really reaching his goals. What is it that you don't respect? Well, in many cases, what you might not respect is his lack of awareness that he is not well suited to the job. It is hard to watch your partner continue to do something in earnest while he remains seemingly unaware he is on the wrong path for himself. On the other hand, a problem can arise if your partner loves doing something and is fairly successful at it, but you don't think it's particularly interesting, and you can't understand why on earth your partner would want to do this job. Either way, you are faced with a dilemma: Do I just accept this aspect of my partner, look past it, and emphasize all the good things I like about him in the relationship, or do I confront him on this issue?

In my experience, issues in a relationship that cause you to lose respect for your partner must be addressed. This is because lack of respect in a relationship sometimes points to inherent incompatibilities in our personalities. Of course, one always wants to bring up such an issue with a tremendous amount of sensitivity. Before bringing it up, you should make certain it is truly your intention to try to understand why your partner is doing what they're doing and why they feel it is a good fit for them. It is possible that you do not have clarity on the issue and that the new information your partner provides could change your perspective. Maybe, for example, he himself knows he isn't well suited to something but has a particular passion for it and could not fathom doing anything else. If you can't find reasons in the course of your discussion to change your perspective, you need to openly express to your partner that you don't have respect or have lost respect for his career path. This, of course, can be terribly scary, because in being honest, you may feel you risk ending the relationship.

It is always difficult to understand what to accept about your partner and what to challenge him on. However, something as significant as what somebody chooses to do with most of his waking time during the week and what motivates his professional life simply cannot be overlooked. If you engage in a dialogue about it, you will learn much more about yourself and your partner and build the muscles necessary to withstand conflict in a relationship, whether or not the two of you decide to stay together.

Do you respect your partner's job and career path?

― 14 ―

If you think that she will change her mind in time, be careful

Many of us end up in a difficult situation with our partners. We love them very much, appreciate many of their great qualities and attributes, and feel that, in many ways, they are an excellent match. However, there may be a few sticking points that create significant conflict and keep us up at night. He may not really want children. She may hate to travel. He may not value a clean home. These issues are possible deal breakers and need to be taken very seriously. They are often deeply connected to a person's self-image: "I am just not the kind of guy who keeps a clean home; I worry about more important things," or "I don't believe in bringing children into this cruel world."

You should not expect his beliefs to change through coercion or gentle persuasion over time. Although some of these beliefs may change eventually, this change isn't something you can count on. If you and your partner are at an impasse on a crucial issue—such as whether or not to have children—I advise you to seek professional assistance. The clearer you are with your partner about what's negotiable and what's not, the sooner you can determine whether your relationship has a future.

Do you agree with your mate on issues like having children, religion, or travel? If not, are you hoping he will change?

— 15 —

Don't wait forever for progress in the relationship on issues that are important to you

The flip side of impatience is misplaced wishful thinking. When you love someone a lot, you want to believe that the problems in your relationship will eventually work themselves out. Unfortunately, this is not likely to happen. A general law of human behavior is that if individuals do not exert significant effort on a regular basis to change themselves, they will stay the same. Although it is unrealistic to expect change overnight, it is possible to measure change in years or even months. If there is little to no progress in the areas of concern over the span of a year, then your relationship needs serious reevaluating.

When you identify an area in which little progress is being made, the first step is to have a dialogue with your partner about why there has been a lack of effort or a lack of recognition that these issues are important to you. Then it will be up to you to evaluate the answers your partner gives you. Do they seem to be the same old excuses, or does your partner show increased awareness of why he feels stuck in his efforts to work on these areas? If this conversation stimulates movement toward change, that's wonderful. If it does not, you may need to consider seeing a therapist together to explore why there as been no progress. Either way, you're in a better position if you understand that change doesn't happen by accident. Always talk about the issues, and show empathy and understanding with your partner, but don't wait forever.

> *Do you find yourself wishing that your partner would work on important relationship issues, but never see any consistent motivation or progress?*

– 16 –

If you have sexual issues that are not going away, a little help can make all the difference

Few issues are more disheartening and depressing in a relationship than sexual problems that don't resolve themselves over time. More than a few times, I've heard from a couple, "Everything is great. We love each other very much. But if our sexual issues don't get resolved, I just don't see how we can stay together." In these situations, a therapist may be necessary to provide the insight and pragmatic advice to help the couple make progress. Many unresolved sexual issues arise from a lack of information rather than a deeply ingrained dysfunction. Couples are often amazed to learn that good sex takes work. Many people have never discussed the sensitive issues surrounding sexuality with anyone in their lives, except casually with close friends. However, in the course of an intimate relationship, sexuality can become more complex. Often these couples will feel hopeless and blame themselves for not figuring it out.

The first thing I would want any couple to know is that they are not alone in confronting these common issues. If you feel that your relationship is wonderful and that the only problem keeping you from taking the next step is a sexual one, seek guidance. Remember, you are not the only couple dealing with this issue, and it may very well resolve itself with a little help in a short period of time. You'll be surprised at how a little shift in your approach can bring quick resolution to what may feel like an intractable problem. Stay optimistic and seek help. There is a great chance you'll move past this impasse and experience sexual intimacy that fulfills you and your partner now and in the future.

Do either of you feel like it's not working sexually?

~ 17 ~

Patience is a virtue. No, really, it is

In our modern, information-on-demand society, patience is an endangered species. We live in a medium of instant gratification: BlackBerrys, iPhones, instant messaging, constant e-mails back and forth, and 1,000 TV channels. You can buy or sell anything you want immediately, and anything you want within reason is instantly within your reach. This immediate gratification—the instant availability of material goods, information, and services—actually weakens our "patience muscles." This means that our ability to wait, delay our needs, and allow ourselves to grasp patterns over time is deeply compromised. As a result, individuals often end up making hasty, uninformed decisions in both the material and the interpersonal realm.

For example, if you aren't getting what you want emotionally from your partner right now, do you feel intense frustration or guilt? Do you contemplate breaking up and meeting someone new on the Internet? Or do you lash out at your partner in anger and judgment? Along these lines, there is a point that all couples reach—maybe very soon after meeting, maybe after a course of months or even years—but reach inevitably. This point is the moment when you begin to realize that not all your needs are going to be met by your mate in the manner you wanted them to be. This may include needs that are physical, sexual, and financial or in other areas of communication and intimacy. One can hope that there are also many needs that are getting met, and that is why you are still together.

One important consideration: Have you spoken about these areas of dissatisfaction and attempted to address them? If you have, that's great. If not, give it a try. If you feel the parts that need to change are very important to you, but you do have a very good relationship in general, have patience. Work with your partner on these issues, and measure your progress on them over the course of months or even years, not ten days or ten weeks.

True and lasting change takes time. As long as you both feel committed to the process of working on your issues, you have excellent prospects for your future. Your patience will pay off, and you will find yourself, many years from now, in awe of how much your relationship has changed for the better.

> *Are you looking for a "quick fix" to conflicts in your relationship?*

~ 18 ~

How do you feel about family and children?

The decision to get engaged is putting you on a path toward marriage and possibly children. Your views and your future spouse's views on the importance of family should be compatible. You should discuss your feelings about having children and becoming a part of your partner's family. Understanding your own place in your partner's preexisting template of familial relationships will help you to understand the challenges each of you may face upon entering each other's family. For example, did your partner have a close family with warm relationships, or was there a lot of conflict and disconnection?

Discussing the issue of having children someday is also tremendously important. This does not mean you have to have an ironclad contract in terms of when, how many, and what gender. But you do have to talk honestly and openly about what your current feelings are regarding kids. What this discussion will do is provide you with some intuitive feeling regarding whether the two of you are basically on the same page. If you are, that's great. If you are not, keep talking about it. Rather than debate the relative merits of one view or another, try to use the discussion to gain a clearer understanding of the differences in opinion. If you find that despite continued discussion you are unable to resolve the issue, you may have a problem on your hands. Either your partner genuinely wants a life very different from the one you want regarding family and children, or he is blocked in some way emotionally and has some work to do in order to resolve feelings about his own family and childhood.

Whatever the case may be, at this point, it may be appropriate to consult a therapist to try to help both of you gain greater clarity regarding why your partner holds the particular views he or she does. Either way, always strive to gain a better understanding of each other instead of attempting to avoid the conflict or "win" the conflict. This is the only way to make a truly informed decision about the viability of your relationship.

> *Do you have unresolved conflict with your partner about family or children?*

~ 19 ~

Be open to discussing your family's problems—you've probably inherited some of them anyway

Most of us are fiercely loyal to our families and will defend them from any criticism. This kind of defense is only natural and is understandable on many levels. It is something we develop at a very young age in order to maintain our sense of integrity as a family unit. Understandably, we may take criticism of our family very personally and feel bad for our parents or siblings. In some cases, even our defensive stance about our families arose from the pain of how flawed or problematic they really were. As we mature into adulthood, however, this instinctive defensiveness can leave us blind to some of our own issues. This usually leads to significant problems for a couple.

Those who have a particularly painful family history may carry a lot of shame, consciously or unconsciously. Shame may be the most difficult emotion to share with another person. It may even feel too unsafe to discuss your past in detail. In this case, it might be appropriate to seek out a therapist to help you work through some of these issues so that you can become more comfortable bringing them up with your significant other. The process of understanding each other's families can bring about much-needed clarity as you embark on your own journey toward marriage and family. The more information you have about your own patterns as shaped by your family history, as well as the patterns of your partner, the better equipped you'll be for the inevitable difficulties that stem from being a part of each other's families, and the less likely you'll be to replicate some of these unhealthy patterns when you create your own.

Though it may be painful to hear from an outsider, denying the reality of your family's issues will always lead to problems in your relationship and in the family you will create together someday. It may be difficult at first, but you must find the courage to explore your own familial imperfections and issues. You will then be able to understand whether you are at risk of repeating the same patterns in your own relationship. Your openness to discussing these issues with your partner will also create a greater feeling of trust and intimacy.

Have you discussed, openly and honestly, your feelings about your and your partner's family issues and problems?

~ 20 ~

You're going to have to deal with your future in-laws whether you love them or not

Our popular culture is filled with jokes about the in-laws. Hollywood is not entirely mistaken in this case. When you choose your partner, you've also indirectly chosen to be with her parents, brothers, sisters, cousins, and others. Families come in different sizes, with different cultures and different styles of interaction. You may be thrilled to discover how well you get along with them, or you may be frustrated by how impossible it is for you to connect with them. Sometimes, you may find there is at least one in-law whom you don't get along with easily yet will need to interact with at family occasions. The engagement party or wedding will likely be the first of many such family get-togethers. It is best to share your feelings about her family with your partner, even regarding those members you aren't crazy about. She needs to know where you're coming from, even if the two of you disagree about certain people. This way, you can work as a team to address family issues that arise.

When you are having this conversation, remain empathic and sensitive to your partner's feelings because they are sure to be complex when family is concerned. Although she may agree with your assessment of certain individuals, she may have a harder time setting boundaries with people she loves and grew up with. On the other hand, she may be able to point out positive characteristics in a family member you dislike and provide you an unexpected opportunity to connect with that person. If you approach your mate with respect and understanding, you will find ways to handle the situation together.

> *Is there anyone in your partner's family with whom you don't get along?*

~ 21 ~

Religion is not unimportant

Many couples feel that their love and connection to one another will surmount all foreseeable obstacles. These individuals should be applauded for their passion, and in many cases a loving and strongly connected couple is able to weather most challenges and come away stronger, wiser, and closer. Yet there are certain topics and issues that won't affect a couple fully until they make the decision to have children. One such issue is religion. Some feel that marrying someone of the same faith is a must, but many couples seem to think their connectedness and willingness to stay together at any cost will surely trump issues so potentially divisive as religious differences. Nations themselves are quick to war over issues like religion, so it is no surprise that couples choose to put off discussions of the nuts and bolts of their own religious practices until a pressing need arises (such as children). These people run the risk of blindsiding each other with what may be very different ideologies and practices.

Religious sensibility tends to be deeply ingrained in our individual identities because we usually receive our most intense exposure to our family's religion when we are quite young. Later, in our adolescent and adult lives, we come to make our own decisions about what these traditions mean to us, though by this time, their basic tenets, rituals, and mythologies are already part of us. Whether someone has been raised with a strong religious faith in God, has had a more secular religious experience, or is an atheist, such views generally remain a very important part of that person's sense of self. Even if a person is set against a particular spiritual tradition, it still may be a factor influencing his religious leanings or spirituality, if only as a set of ideas to react against.

Sometimes religious issues come up while a couple is dating, during the holidays, or while planning the wedding. But most of the intense conflict over religion that I see in couples revolves around raising children. No matter the situation prompting the discussion, the open and honest review of your respective religious identities can help your partner discover important aspects of you, and is yet another wonderful way to get to know your partner's layered personality. If you have this discussion early on, you can defuse the potentially explosive conflicts that are certain to come once children are in the picture.

Have you sat down and discussed how religion and your respective religious beliefs will affect your marriage and how you raise your children?

— 22 —

Marriage is also a business. Money is a real issue

The issue of money may not seem significant in the beginning of a relationship, but you will eventually have to address it. On the path toward engagement, you should have a sober discussion about finances. Couples come up with different ways of handling finances. Some will merge their accounts, others will keep them completely separate, and many find an arrangement that is somewhere in between. When you share a life, what you spend money on and how freely you do so may differ. That is why it is always important to share your ideas and goals regarding finances. You will want to look at your spending and saving habits to see whether you are on the same page. Having these conversations as you get engaged is a good idea. You don't want to wait too long. I have worked with too many couples who realized only after getting married that they are on opposite ends of the spectrum in their financial habits and values.

How much debt do you or your partner have? What assets are you bringing to the table? How do you feel about sharing the money you have earned? What do you and your partner enjoy spending money on? What are your goals surrounding home ownership and long-term material possessions? These questions can be a point of contention for many couples, so by asking them early on, you won't feel surprised and resentful later. If you discuss and deal with these issues in a grounded and sensitive way, you will establish good patterns for your future life together. This will allow you to support each other in times of stress, and you'll ultimately be more likely to develop a system of handling your finances that will allow you to feel closer and share your financial ups and downs as a team.

Have you discussed how much financial debt you and your partner have, and do you have the same ideas about how to spend and save money?

— 23 —

We are not created equal. Be aware of your differences

People often make the mistake of confusing "equal" with "the same." We are all, of course, equal as human beings, worthy of equal respect, love, and kindness. However, we are not the same in terms of innate temperaments, abilities, strengths, weaknesses, and viewpoints. This is crucial to understand, especially in an intimate relationship. I see couples continually make the mistake of believing their partner should respond to them in exactly the same way they themselves would respond given a similar situation. It is an all-too-common error to view your partner as flawed if he responds differently to a conflict than you would. You may think he is the less attuned, less nice, less understanding version of yourself. This mistake ultimately leads to an intense misunderstanding and, on the part of your partner, the feeling of being judged. You can quite easily prevent these situations from arising by trying to get a clear understanding of ways in which you and your partner are very different people.

Take some time and think about how well you and your partner know each other. In which areas do you share traits, and how are you different? In the gray areas where you feel you and your partner are not on the same page, you may believe he is wrong and needs to change, or you might instead value his differing perspective. Also, when you look at your partner's communication style and how it differs from yours, do you view his as inadequate and misguided? Or does he have an equally valid style but takes a different road?

I am not suggesting that your differences are all valuable assets to a relationship. He really may not communicate well, and you may need to address this as a real problem in the relationship. She may hold views on finances or politics that feel too rigid for your world view. One of you may feel at sea with personal finances or have poor organizational skills. Each individual in the relationship brings a variety of perspectives and abilities to the table. Each of these differences makes up an ingredient in a complex meal. It is the unique balance of these ingredients that produces a superb dish.

Not all foods and spices are meant to be combined. However, if you do a careful study of the varied ingredients, you will be in an excellent position to know if you have the right recipe. Please take both time and effort in evaluating the differences and similarities you have with your partner. This way you can make an open, honest assessment of which traits to value and respect, and in turn, which behaviors need to change. You will thereby give yourself the best opportunity for a successful relationship built on harmonious similarities and complementary differences.

> *Do you find yourself wishing that your partner was more like you?*

− 24 −

Get off your high horse

We can get really angry when we feel hurt, misunderstood, or betrayed by our partner. These feelings—shame, fear, intense anger—cut to the bone. When such intense feelings arise, many people react outwardly by withdrawing and shutting down or by lashing out aggressively. Others may loudly proclaim their outrage at what someone else has said or done, insisting they themselves would never have said or done such a thing. Of course, the most destructive response is when someone throws a tantrum, denouncing his partner as a horrible person. Needless to say, these ways of handling emotional wounds do not tend to lead to good outcomes in a relationship. I would like to propose a very different approach.

As soon as you find yourself assembling your troops to attack, or planning to withdraw, take a moment and pause. Breathe and ponder something: Have you never been hurtful or said something thoughtless to your partner or, for that matter, to anyone? If the answer is that you never have, then you should be canonized for sainthood and become a missionary, because the world needs you more than your partner does.

For the rest of us, the answer will be that of course we have, and, more likely than not, many times. This simple insight serves to impart an empathic understanding of how someone you love so much, and who professes to love you so much in return, could hurt you so seemingly thoughtlessly. In response, then, you can simply communicate, "I felt hurt that you did this and said that and I don't want you to do it again," or, "I don't understand, and I would like you to explain your actions to me."

It takes great courage and discipline to open your heart and communicate respectfully while in pain. However, this is ultimately the only way to build the trust and security that you both need to grow closer together.

Do you feel superior or self-righteous when you are disappointed or hurt by your partner?

─ 25 ─

If you really knew me, you would never hurt me

We all want to be understood, "gotten," heard, and empathized with. This desire is arguably the most important need we have as human beings. It is this impulse that pushes us to reach out, socialize, connect, and ultimately commit to a long-term relationship. Even when couples seem to be immersed in never-ending conflict and difficulty, many will struggle and "hang in there" for years and years for this simple reason: "Nobody knows me like my partner does." This internal narrative continues: "We have a history, and I can't believe anyone will ever know me or understand me equally well." Whether or not this self-assessment is accurate is open to question, but the fear of not being understood ever again in life is undeniable and, for many of us, terrifying.

In the beginning of a relationship, this feeling of being gotten is indescribably wonderful. In fact, this may be one of the chief attractions a couple feels for each other. However, as time moves on, the unrealistic expectation of perfect attunement is broken. The experience of hurt in this moment is somewhat tragic. The dawning realization that this person may also hurt and misunderstand you, just as others have, is truly sad. Our immediate response to this pain is often something along the lines of, "If you really cared about me or loved me, you would not have made this mistake and misunderstood me in this way. If you really knew me, you would never hurt me." Alas, most of us, if not all of us, are not mind readers, and even the best of us, the most empathic, will make mistakes.

If you really want your partner to know you more and more and to understand you in a way that almost seems like mind reading, you must talk to them when you feel hurt or misunderstood, difficult though this may be at times. In this process of hurt, communication, and healing, you will grow closer to each other than you would have imagined possible.

> *Do you doubt your compatibility when your partner disappoints you?*

~ 26 ~

Talk about the little issues or they will grow into big issues

One common misconception about good communication is the idea that you should always let the little things go. When something small comes up, why is it that we don't want to make a big deal of it? Well, we don't want to be seen as being too picky and critical. Also, we don't want to feel that we are over-analyzing everything and magnifying problems. I say, don't let these opportunities pass you by.

I would like to introduce the "little deal." The more little deals you and your partner bring up and work through, the better off you will be. Each small issue that presents itself is an opportunity to explore your internal baggage and, in turn, to recognize how it is affecting your current relationship. Working out the lesser problems also dispels fear of conflict or rejection. This will build up your "conflict muscles" and make you stronger and more experienced so that you will be able to successfully deal with the big issues. Having opened up areas of hurt for discussion also brings about greater intimacy.

The process of deciding whether or not to bring up a little deal can be tricky. It's easy for us to say to ourselves, "It doesn't matter!" Most of us will need to push ourselves to open up about these little deals. Once you bring them up, though, you will find, if you have a willing partner, that these issues can be resolved quite quickly.

Do you find yourself letting little things go by that cause resentment down the road?

$-27-$

Don't express every random thought that you have in your head about your partner

This may seem deceptively obvious, but it might surprise you how much it can help in a relationship to filter your communication. Some people feel that, because they are in an intimate relationship, they have the right to express themselves, whenever, for whatever reason. This idea is an outsized version of the healthy desire not to shut yourself down and hold things back. One may have even come from a childhood where self-expression was stifled and discouraged. That person will react particularly strongly to suggestions that filtering and timing his thoughts about you is important. However, we must remember that in a mature relationship, your first and foremost goal is to learn how to continue to build upon your ability to communicate effectively. And in this vein, one of the most important things to learn about communication is appropriate timing and context.

You want to ask yourself, Have I thought through what I want to express to my partner, or is this the first time it has come to my mind? Is this issue relatively simple, or is this issue highly sensitive? It's surprising how rarely a person considers these sorts of questions before discussing issues with the partner. Yet the same individual will often ask themselves these questions, along with many others, before discussing highly sensitive issues with a boss, friend, or family member. I believe this has something to do with the misconception that we have the right to express ourselves however we want with our significant others. It's a belief that is based on the idea that our partner should be available at all times to discuss our feelings about certain subjects, regardless of the emotional state he is in. This is a good time to practice pausing, taking a breath, and empathically considering how you would want him to express his thoughts to you. Furthermore, do you really want him to talk about thoughts he has had about you which are based, not on the reality of your relationship, but rather on his reaction to the stresses he is feeling in his own life?

Become aware of how your emotional state can distort your thoughts about and reactions to your partner. With this increased awareness, you will begin to recognize the patterns of thoughts that tend to come at times of stress, before you rush to verbalize them to your partner unnecessarily. That way, when you do have to communicate something important and sensitive, you can try to pick the best time, frame it in the right way, and, ultimately, have the satisfaction of knowing that you are able to clearly say what you wanted to say.

How much do you consider your emotional state and your partner's before you talk to him?

— 28 —

Couples who don't argue are in trouble

Sometimes, in the privacy of my office, I wonder at our abilities as humans to communicate with one another at all. All of us come from such different families, with different experiences, vastly different temperaments, and incredibly wide-ranging perceptions of the world. In light of such diversity across all spectrums of human experience, how is it we are not miscommunicating with one another constantly?

Most couples go through similar phases in the course of their relationship. In the beginning, there was the excitement of feeling so "right," so understood by the other. At some point or other, this feeling will be rudely interrupted by the first major failure to understand. Your partner will fall short of your expectations in some significant way. This is part of the natural, organic evolution in the course of life, and so too is it part of the natural evolution of a healthy relationship. We hold an image of someone that is two-dimensional and, eventually, life shows us the full reality in all its sometimes less-than-beautiful dimensions. Such a realization may be an unavoidable consequence of learning about each other, though not necessarily an unfortunate one. As we learn more about our partner, we are provided with the opportunity for choice. We can choose, consciously or unconsciously, to "steer clear" of potentially messy aspects of our partner's personality, or we can choose to lean into their discontinuities and roughness and come, perhaps, to connect with them on an altogether more human level.

Many will choose the temporary "feel good" solution and rationalize away their disappointment in their partner. In my experience, those who refuse to see their partner's imperfections will ultimately suffer tremendously. Such couples tend to be afraid to acknowledge the very real problems in their relationships for fear that this is somehow an affirmation they are badly suited to each other. This is an awful predicament: believing fundamentally that if you communicate a problem, argue your position, or express disappointment, your relationship is hopelessly flawed and the two of you are incompatible. The suppression and denial necessary to maintain these beliefs, despite the reality staring you in the face each day, leads to incredible unspoken tension and passive aggressiveness. Ultimately, the relationship becomes little more than a minefield of subjects that can no longer be discussed openly with authentic feeling.

Couples who "agree to never disagree" actually end up hurting both themselves and their relationship significantly and deeply, unlike those who talk openly about their problems. My advice: Closely examine whether you are in some way trying to avoid the reality of your relationship, flaws and all. It's a bit like trying to defy gravity by pretending it isn't there; you can put on a flowing red cape and step out a top-floor window, but you are unlikely to remain aloft for long. Better to be here now, try to work through your problems, and step forward through the fear to argue forcefully for what you believe in. If you do so wholeheartedly and unselfishly, the effort is certain to be a rewarding experience for both of you.

> *Do you find yourself avoiding any and all fights, so that you and your mate hardly ever have a debate or discussion about issues that bother either of you?*

~ 29 ~

The more you yell, the less you will be heard

Anger is unavoidable in any relationship. We certainly don't always see eye to eye with our partners. In addition, we are constantly experiencing shifting feelings about each other, which at times is bound to cause conflict that is not easily resolvable. The most dangerous form of conflict stems from the feeling that you can't make your partner understand or empathize with your position. We have all experienced this kind of situation—we feel anger and hopelessness at the same time. Sometimes the frustration wants to boil over, and we think to ourselves, What do I have to do to make him understand me? The most primitive behavioral response to this internal question is that we say things louder and with a more aggressive tone. Unfortunately, getting louder and louder eventually turns into yelling and will always put your partner in a defensive, threatened position. This greatly increases the chances that he will cease to have any interest in understanding your thoughts or feelings. He will now be completely concerned with his own feelings of being attacked and will either withdraw and shut down or counter by yelling back even louder. I needn't paint a more detailed picture of this scenario, and it leads nowhere good.

Couples who yell at each other cause unnecessary pain and ill will, which destroys a relationship from the inside. We pointedly remember these painful encounters, and they inform our stance in future conflicts. This means that in the next conflict, both partners will harbor residual fear and aggression and, as a result, will be less open, less sympathetic, and less motivated to communicate, a stance that greatly increases the chances of a fight occurring even sooner than it ordinarily would. When enough resentment builds up over time, yelling leads to insults, and insults become curses. In extreme cases, physical abuse can result. This risk of escalation and the guarantee of emotional pain accompanying it are the reasons such patterns are the most destructive we can create in a relationship. If we find ourselves engaging in yelling, insulting, and cursing, we know we have a big problem on our hands. A relationship like this can fall very far, very fast.

If you and your partner are falling into such patterns of interaction regularly, my advice to you is to consult a professional as soon as possible, to avoid doing more damage. No one is perfect, and we all get angry and sometimes lose our self-control. However, these events should be exceptionally rare in a relationship, and the goal is to eliminate them altogether. If you recognize this pattern in time, you can get help and devise more constructive ways to deal with your anger. Remember, it will always be better in the long run to feel the pain of being misunderstood than to feel the shame of having lost your temper and caused your partner equal pain.

> *Do some of your arguments involve yelling, cursing, or insults?*

‒ 30 ‒

Don't compare your partner to someone you both dislike

I know this sounds obvious to anyone reading it right now, but how many of you have more than once said, "Stop treating me like Bob did!" or "That's something your mother would say!" or my favorite, "You are acting really stupid, just like Jim." These kinds of insults really hit us at our core. Comparing someone else's distasteful past actions or patterns to those of your partner is never a constructive way to deal with hurt feelings. Feeling emotionally threatened, we are all quick to defend ourselves in such a situation and fight back. This habit of attacking and counterattacking leads to more distance, hurt, and feelings of isolation and hopelessness. I cannot stress enough how damaging these attacks can be if they are repeated over time. Comments of this stripe belong on an "off-limits" list. Couples who keep an agreed-upon off-limits list in mind are much more likely to take a time-out when they are angry, and not speak until they are calm enough to choose their words carefully and constructively. I suggest sitting down either together or separately and coming up with your own off-limits list. Relationships are hard enough when couples stick to respectful communication. When a couple doesn't, a better relationship is impossible.

Do you or your potential spouse compare the other to a disliked person when in the throes of an argument?

– 31 –

The best couples argue forcefully but with empathy and respect

What is a "good" argument between a couple? I believe knowing how to argue is as important as knowing how to compromise and get along. Most of us are good at getting along with others to some degree and know how to compromise when the stakes are too high. However, if we have received any training whatsoever in the art of arguing, it is usually within the context of forensic debate. Unfortunately, this style of argument is particularly ill suited to intimacy. In a debate, the goal is to win—to beat your opponent with the blunt force and savvy of your reasoning and, in the process, to score more points and be declared the winner. In intimate circumstances, there are no judges, and rarely are points awarded for a dazzling opening or a convincing counterpoint. Instead, feelings are stepped on, and partners are made to feel more distant from each other.

Intimate argument, unlike debate, must involve the mutual acknowledgment of multiple perspectives—not the dogmatic thrust of one particular perspective. What if it happens that your partner feels very strongly about a point of view different from yours? What should your first move be? Well, I can tell you what it should not be: to pick apart and destroy her perspective as ill conceived and irrational. This will not result in points scored but will distance her. Instead of jumping the gun to be right and attempting to establish yourself as the "winner," try asking questions first. This will help you understand exactly where your partner is coming from and the breadth of her perspective. That way, she will feel your respect and genuine interest and will be more inclined to begin to engage in an actual thoughtful dialogue rather than a debate.

In a dialogue there is no winner or loser. Instead, both sides win by getting closer to understanding each other and building upon their mutual sense of trust. This, in turn, makes it easier to confront the more and more difficult issues that will inevitably arise. Furthermore, there is a good chance that through dialogue and not debate, over time, in fits and starts, a novel perspective will emerge that may bring you both to a mutual understanding.

Are you trying to "win" your arguments with your partner?

— 32 —

Never say "you never" or "you always"

A month or so after marriage, my wife and I met an elderly gentleman at a party. He immediately spotted us as newlyweds, holding hands, lovingly attending to each other. He walked slowly over to us with his cane, introduced himself, and asked how long we'd been married. He congratulated us and told us his wife of sixty years had passed away recently. We spoke with him for about five minutes, asking about his wife, when, suddenly, his tone changed. He paused, looked wistfully at us, and said, "I want to give you some advice as a man who was married for sixty years. My wife and I, we argued—we had some really tough times through which we were not sure we would make it. During one of these arguments or fights, as you might call them, my wife pointed out that both she and I were in a nasty habit of saying 'You never do or say this,' or 'You always do or say that!' We realized that this way of speaking to one another, generalizing in this extreme way rather than being specific, always ended up causing us the most hurt." He maintained that from then on, they vowed to try never to use those statements and to communicate about a specific act, without generalizing out of pain or anger. Once they agreed to do this—and it did take them about twenty years to figure this out ("We were a little slow!" he joked)—the next forty years were much smoother sailing. Not perfect, but they were able to get closer and closer, and their love grew with each year. "Good luck!" he said, "and remember: never say 'You never' or 'You always.'"

I can't say my wife and I have followed his advice to the letter. But we really have tried, and we've definitely gotten a lot "better" at arguing! Whenever those words start to cross our lips in an argument, one of us will raise an eyebrow and we will both laugh and remember how wise that man was. We feel very grateful to have met him.

Do either of you use generalized accusations such as "You always . . ." or "You never . . ."?

～ 33 ～

Real people will fall short of your expectations over and over again

One enduring myth many people hold about great relationships is that you don't get hurt or disappointed very much, or even at all. Unfortunately, people will always be people, no matter the situation, no matter the good intentions, no matter the intensity of the chemistry or love. This means that despite how wonderfully well suited you are to your partner, at times you will feel so disappointed and hurt that you will question whether this is the right person for you at all.

What is important to understand is that this is going to happen, so expect it if it hasn't happened already. This way, you will be prepared to talk constructively about your feelings rather than dwelling on how "this isn't how a relationship should be!" If you can start at a place of humble equality with each other, then you will have the background, empathy, and sensitivity necessary to express your hurt in a meaningful way. The goal of any relationship is not to avoid conflict or get rid of conflict, but to continually work to find creative solutions to conflict in an environment of ever-growing trust and security. If you try to remember this in times of despair, it will go a long way to resolving even some of the deepest misgivings and disappointments in a relationship.

> *Do you understand that both you and your partner will fall short of each other's expectations?*

– 34 –

Apologies are golden, but make them real

A real, heartfelt apology is the closest thing we have to a magical power. An apology's ability to heal deep wounds, repair misunderstandings, and close a great distance is awe-inspiring. So why is it that many of us have such trouble making a genuine apology? It's somewhat easy to say, "I'm sorry about this" or "I didn't mean that," but real apologies don't depend so much on specific words or phrases. Real apologies are those in which we take complete responsibility for the hurt we have caused. Most of us have a very hard time taking full responsibility for pain caused to a loved one. Usually we feel we were provoked, so our aggressive response was in some way merited and therefore justified. An eye for an eye. Regardless of provocation, though, it is important to understand that there is no excuse for our own hurtful words and deeds.

Let me give some examples of bad apologies. Can you remember ever having said, "I am sorry you are so sensitive," "I am sorry you feel that way," "I am sorry you are so stupid," and "I am sorry I ever met you"? As you can see from these examples, saying "I am sorry" and then filling in the blank often doesn't cut it. In order to truly repair a hurt and not allow wounds to fester, you must do the following: stand up straight, take a good breath, and say something like "I am really sorry for saying that to you"—no excuses, no fear. "I was wrong to do it and will do everything in my power to remember not to do it again. I hope you can forgive me." That's a real take-no-prisoners apology, and there is real relationship-healing magic in it.

Of course, such an apology is easier to plan than to execute. If it weren't, we would all be doing it all the time! My advice: Start with the simple things, the little things, and build up the "muscle of apology." Then, when you really need that muscle to be strong, it will be there for the really important situations to come.

> *Do you have difficulty taking full responsibility*
> *when you apologize?*

~ 35 ~

Apologies are incomplete without a change in behavior

Giving and receiving apologies is an integral part of any relationship. Apologies allow us to recognize our imperfections and repair hurt feelings. The most crucial aspect of an apology is the subsequent change in behavior by the one who has apologized. People often complain that their spouse makes a heartfelt statement of remorse and then continues exhibiting the objectionable behavior. When this happens, a discussion is needed. Without making a concerted effort to change his behavior through increased awareness, the hurt between you cannot be mended.

If you witness in your potential spouse an inability or lack of desire to grow, even at the expense of your wounded feelings, then you have a problem. At this point, you would be well advised to seek professional help in order to gain greater clarity into why your partner's behavior has not improved. You can only hope that your partner will be able to uncover why he has been incapable of following through on his apology. Regardless of the outcome, you will, at least, get real and be in a more secure position to decide whether your relationship has a future.

Do either of you chronically make apologies that aren't followed up with a change in behavior?

Everyone doubts at one time or another whether his partner is "the one"

Let's begin with an analysis of this concept of "the one." Where do we come by this idea, and what does it really mean in our society? "The one" has an almost messianic, religious flavor to it—the savior, the perfect mate, the one who will make all my loneliness go away and make me happy forever. How do we know who "the one" might be? Is there some secret formula or some esoteric mystical understanding that will lead us to know whether a particular person meets the requirements?

Most of us do not consciously think this way, but this image of "the one" is such a common theme in our society that it always lurks in the background of a relationship. It raises the stakes of making a mistake and ending up with a person who is destined to be not "the one" but rather "the wrong one." Everyone doubts at some point whether or not she has made the right choice. I would like to encourage you to reevaluate this largely media-driven image of "the one." First, it is highly unlikely that there is only one, perfectly compatible, right person in the world for you. Second, because even those who are compatible with us will sometimes hurt and disappoint us, anyone can make you doubt the rightness of the match.

This doubt is not a problem; it is a healthy response to areas of incompatibility and misunderstanding. In fact, if this doubt comes after a series of repeated hurts, then it is a very important perspective that can lead to greater clarity. One can hope that this doubt will lead you to take stock of the relationship, address the issues head-on, and find out whether your partner really is capable of meeting your needs. This is what I call healthy doubt, and it leads to greater dialogue and the possibility of creating a truly nourishing relationship.

Unhealthy doubt is that which comes from the concept of "the one." This is a chronic doubt, a critical voice you hear every time you feel that you and your partner have experienced conflict. This kind of doubt leads a person to withdraw, sulk, feel hopeless, and begin to question every aspect of the relationship. This response is often a misunderstanding. It comes from the idea that "the one" would never cause you any of these negative feelings. Please take solace in knowing that even the most wonderfully compatible and nurturing partners are not always there for each other. They, too, misunderstand each other and feel hopeless at times. Better then to save the idea of "the one" for the spiritual realm, where it belongs. In looking for a partner, remember along the way that she will most likely turn out to be a complicated human being just like you.

> *Do you have "healthy doubt" or "unhealthy doubt" about your partner being well suited to you?*

– 37 –

Everyone goes through dark times in a relationship

It is how you handle the tough times within your marriage that will define you as a couple. People often say, "Relationships should not be this difficult!" For the word "relationships," you may as well substitute "work," "parenthood," "friendship," or "life." And yet, anyone who has achieved any success in any of these realms will tell you that it is supposed to be hard. In order to reap great rewards, you must put in a great amount of effort, patience, and creativity. Accepting this reality will give you the strength to work through these times.

Too often, a couple responds to a crisis in the relationship by doubting their compatibility. Doubt only leads to more uncertainty. Clarity only comes through dealing with the crisis head-on and seeing whether the two of you can work through it successfully. The courage needed to face tough times together is admirable, and it never comes easy.

Remember that you are not alone. Everyone in every relationship has to commit to learning and growing if he wants to surmount the challenges that will inevitably come. The sooner you adopt this perspective, the more prepared you will be to get the most out of every difficult encounter that life throws your way.

Do you recognize that any couple that has been together for a long time has had dark times they had to work through?

– 38 –

It's normal to feel attracted to someone who's not your partner

As human beings and as sexual beings, we will find ourselves attracted to other people besides our partner throughout the course of our life together. This feeling of attraction is natural. It is part of being a living, vital, sexual person. The important thing to know is what to do with this feeling of vitality and attraction and how to interpret it. Not all attractions mean the same thing, and it is important to distinguish their meanings. When you find yourself attracted to people who meet your eye occasionally, don't judge yourself and feel guilty. This is a completely normal and healthy experience.

Alternatively, if you find yourself seeking out and savoring this type of attraction to other people, it means that you are probably lacking something in your own relationship. You need to get clear about what it is your relationship is lacking and address it. If you find yourself trying to get to know people you find attractive outside the relationship, again, you have a problem. So, it is not the fact of being attracted to someone other than your partner that is a problem; it is acting on that attraction that matters. If you find yourself losing attraction for your partner, you must address that issue immediately. Feeling attracted to other people does not mean there is something wrong with your relationship as long as you remain attracted to your significant other and focused on the well-being of your relationship.

Do you know that it is perfectly normal for you or your mate to find someone else attractive without acting on it?

~ 39 ~

Attracted to another person? Don't put yourself in harm's way

Most of us believe that we will never cheat on our partner. We feel a strong moral sentiment that this is wrong, and we have no desire for it. If you feel this way, that is a great starting place toward remaining faithful to your partner. However, we must acknowledge that we are all human, prone to temptation, at least in part, and, in the wrong situation, we can all make poor decisions and delude ourselves. It makes sense, then, to come up with some commonsense boundaries for our behavior with attractive individuals outside our relationship.

First and most important, be honest with yourself: if you feel attracted to someone you know at work or from another situation, acknowledge it. It is completely natural to have feelings of attraction for people other than your partner. As human animals, we're programmed to have chemistry with certain people, and it's important for you to see it so that you can manage it. Both you and your partner should recognize this reality. If you do, you are less likely to put yourself in compromising situations. For instance, don't go out for a drink with that especially attractive person, since alcohol is the number-one offender in impairing our judgment and making us give in to our baser instincts. Also, make sure you don't take business trips alone with this particular person if the person is, say, a colleague at work. By extension, if you absolutely cannot avoid going on a business trip with your crush, make sure you focus on work and don't spend a lot of time with that person in activities unrelated to work. Definitely avoid late nights at work with this person. Fatigue, like alcohol, is another culprit that can lower your defenses and impair judgment.

The subtlest issue is how and when you spend time with the particular person you're attracted to who isn't your partner. You don't want to innocently start increasing the time with him and then, before you know it, build a deep emotional connection to him. This can happen quite suddenly, so be careful. Healthy people always put structures in place to make sure that they stay safe and healthy, both physically and emotionally.

Acknowledging your vulnerability is a strength, not a weakness. Although some pretend to be above it all, those who turn a blind eye to their human nature are the ones who will end up with the greater difficulties. So be smart: see your vulnerability and attend to it by setting reasonable boundaries. Ultimately, this will allow you to develop your mutual trust and put your energies into the relationship instead of outside it.

Are you attracted to someone outside the relationship and are you finding ways to spend more time with that person?

～ 40 ～

The truth of the moment is not the whole truth

What is the truth, the emotional truth about my partner? Finding an answer to this question is a bit complicated. The reason for this is that our moods shift frequently, our lives are constantly changing, and so are our feelings about our significant other. Maybe, for example, I wake up next to my partner feeling loving and grateful, very much in love. By mid-morning, I may be stressed out by a work project, and she may call and ask me questions I have little patience for under the circumstances. I could react with annoyance. These feelings may pass soon, and by lunchtime I recognize I was stressed, my annoyance emerged from that stress, and I now feel connected once again. In the afternoon, we meet for coffee, and the conversation is less than thrilling; not bad, just a bit dull. This encounter may make me feel sad and concerned about whether we are really connecting anymore. At dinner time, I arrive home only to be surprised with a beautiful meal, hugs, and kisses, and I feel absorbed in feelings of love, arousal, and relief—we are O.K. after all. Now, which of these moments is key? On which experience should I hang my hat and say that this emotion defines our relationship? Of course, none of them is the whole truth. Each feeling, though it may overpower you, though it may feel like the truth and lead you to communicate positively or negatively in a relationship, is still not really defining.

In a strange way, this recognition provides relief. It allows us to detach a bit from the everyday emotional landscape of our interactions with our partner. If we know not to take anyone's momentary sense of reality too seriously, including our own, we can get on with our day and allow ourselves to see the broader picture.

Think of evaluating the truth of your relationship the way you would evaluate a long vacation overseas: When you come back, what do you tell people when they ask you how it was? Do you describe it as great, good, or bad? Do you say, "I'm not sure I would go back," or "I can't wait to return"? We answer this question instinctively and quite quickly because we have some intuitive sense of the whole experience. Looking back on the trip, if we wrote about it extensively, we would find that it consisted of ever-changing emotional states: good, bad, and indifferent. All these emotions combine to create a picture, a representation of the whole. You have a sense of this representation, and you can feel it quite strongly even though during the trip you felt many different emotions. Often this sense of clarity will come in moments of quiet reflection on your way home. This sort of contemplative place is where you need to be to feel out the "truth" of your relationship.

So remember, you may feel gravely conflicting emotions toward your partner within a day and certainly within a week. However, if you take the time to quietly reflect, you are more likely to gain an overall sense of the truth of your relationship as a whole.

Does your general feeling about your relationship shift from day to day?

— 41 —

Marriage doesn't have magical powers to make problems go away

Many times, people dissatisfied with aspects of their relationships come to me insisting things will change after marriage: "He'll be more committed." "We will both want similar things." "We will work harder on our issues." Unfortunately, in most cases marriage offers no such immediate transformation. Although some individuals may feel more safe and secure in a marriage, some may feel less so. We all grow up in institutions: schools, families, sports teams, and so forth. All of these institutions have established rules with clear consequences if the rules are broken. As children, we learn what these boundaries are, and we adjust our behaviors accordingly. In the best institutions, these perimeters allow us to find our freedom. We experience within them the balance between exploration and stability that allows us to grow and expand without hurting others. Sometimes, though, when they do not match well with our deepest intuition and sense of self, these boundaries can exert a destructive influence on our lives.

As impulsive children, we need adults to help us differentiate between what we want and what we need. This mirrors a particular predicament of the institution of marriage. Some people view marriage as a place of safety and stability, while others see marriage as a place of instability and betrayal. The latter cling to a passionate resolve never to submit to what feels like a jail sentence. They would much rather remain in a committed relationship without ever getting married. Often, but not always, these people come from a family environment in which their parents' marriage was an unending cycle of betrayal, hurt, and even abuse. On the other hand, the former often grew up with parents who exemplified a healthy marital relationship. These people desire to attain that kind of deep emotional bond with someone in their own lives. They see the commitment to marriage as a statement that they are worthy of being loved long-term. Such people are in danger of glossing over immediate problems with their beloved once they have assumed the title of "spouse." They cling to their positive preconceived notions of what a spouse is instead of looking at the real person. The initial desire for commitment may have created so much anxiety that, once they are married, the release of stress can bring about an almost magical euphoria. The hope is that once a person has experienced the positive feelings brought on by having signed a marriage license and undergone the commitment ceremony, she will allow this newfound sense of safety to provide the foundation for growth. Along these lines, the confidence of a newlywed can open her mind to exploring her relationship more deeply and to embracing the challenges that arise.

Remember to hold in mind the bedrock notion that change for the better requires honesty and hard work. Then you are free to enjoy your engagement while keeping both feet on the ground. If you remain true to yourself and your partner, you will come to know each other more deeply than anyone else in the world, and a kind of magic, born of this mutual understanding, will be present in your marriage.

> *Are there things about your relationship that you think marriage is going to solve?*

– 42 –

Don't think that having children is going to make it better

Some people consider having children quite soon after marriage, while others tend to wait. If you are among the former, this chapter will be of particular interest to you. For others, it is something to keep in mind for the future. Some couples believe that children will fill a void in the relationship. Let me be clear: children are absolutely a possibility for positive change in the dynamic between married individuals. However, having kids can also be a stressor. They can heighten problems that previously existed. You need to ask yourselves, How do both of us tend to deal with new challenges in our lives?

One can hope that the arrival of children in your lives will cause you to grow closer, but it is also likely at times to cause you to feel overwhelmed and disconnected. The experience of raising a child can bring you incredible joy and profoundly change you for the better. It can also be frustrating and fill your days with unpredictable challenges. The true test, though, will be for you and your partner to respond to these challenges in ways that bring an ever-deepening sense of intimacy and mutual understanding.

> *Do you imagine that having children will make your relationship and marriage better?*

~ 43 ~

Your relationship should not be your only passion in life

I have seen too many people make their relationship the consuming purpose and passion of their life. It always ends in disappointment. Why do so many people seem to do this in the beginning stages of their relationship? It feels so good to be constantly with this new and exciting person. Who wouldn't want to keep that feeling going as long as possible? To a certain degree, this makes sense and is the natural beginning of a romantic partnership. At first your partner will love and appreciate and focus all his attention on you. However, if this intensity continues, it will wreak havoc on your relationship and life. In time, that person will start to look like a one-trick pony without much to offer you personally except his admiration. If that person doesn't have other passions in his life, such as work, hobbies, and other friendships, you will start to feel the pressure of the imbalance.

In many cases, this misdirected passion is the expression of a person with a lot of intelligence, creativity, and energy who just hasn't found his purpose in life yet. You do not want to become that person's purpose! If, in turn, you find yourself losing any sense of yourself for the sake of your beloved, take a step back and get some perspective. Push yourself to try to experiment with some things you like outside of your relationship. Take an art class, listen to new music, or find a sport or physical activity you can get excited about. Finding things of real interest to you and committing to them makes you a more interesting and creative person to yourself and to your partner.

Is your relationship your only passion in life?

― 44 ―

Cultivate your friendships

Friends are a source of tremendous support and strength while you are married. They provide different perspectives and give you an opportunity to share emotions, both joyous and painful, that arise during the course of your marriage. Finding the time to keep up your friendships and establish new ones during a marriage can be quite challenging. Most of us work long hours trying to pay the bills and advance our careers, and your free time is usually reserved for your spouse and children if you have them. The danger in this is that if you relegate your free time exclusively to your spouse and children, you risk living only in three restricted parts of yourself: the work self, the spouse self, and the parent self. These are all important, but they are far from the complete picture of your being.

Consider the fact that for most of your life, your primary role has been that of friend. Most of our time growing up was spent in school or engaged in after-school activities. These were experiences we shared exclusively with friends. We may have dated in high school and college, and yet this was the period in our lives when we formed intense, lasting friendships that have been far more stable than any of those early romantic relationships. When we enter into a long-term relationship and then a marriage, many of us transfer the locus of our emotional support entirely onto our partners. This is natural, especially in the beginning of a relationship, but if it stays this way, it will lead to an imbalance. This is because one of your friends' greatest contributions is to tell you how it really is, to be honest with you without worrying about the ramifications of your response.

A common complaint I hear from troubled couples is, "If only my husband were like my friends, he would always understand me and we could work through any difficulty." This is an astute observation that many of us can identify with. However, our friends are not so intimately entwined in every aspect of our lives. We don't share a home with them, we don't share responsibilities such as cooking, cleaning, finances and budgeting, and, of course, we don't share sex. These aspects of a relationship will enrich you as a couple but also are areas in which there can be far more conflict than in a friendship. That is why having supportive friends outside the relationship is so crucial. These relationships can be much simpler than our intimate ones.

I encourage you to think of your support system as a financial portfolio. You may fall in love with one stock and believe that it will give you all you need, but that hardly ever turns out to be the case. A far better strategy is to keep your support portfolio diversified so that when dividends are not available in one place, they may accrue someplace else. Then, when you have difficulties, you always have a place to turn and perhaps a source of some new perspective outside of your marriage.

> *Do you continue to keep up with friends outside of your relationship?*

~ 45 ~

Couples who share activities are closer

This one may seem obvious to most people. Couples who interact with each other through shared activities have greater intimacy, feelings of partnership, physical attraction, and respect. One of the reasons for this is that we get to know our partners much better through these kinds of activities. Shared activities can include sports, dancing, volunteering, camping, playing games—all involve sophisticated levels of communication. In these low-pressure situations, we may experience conflict and can work to resolve such issues within the appropriate boundaries of the activity.

Shared experiences teach a few important skills. First, they allow you to keep practicing your methods of communication and conflict-resolution in a benign setting. These kinds of positive experiences serve to build a real feeling of trust and closeness in a couple. Second, they also tend to be fun and create positive emotions. This enjoyment leads to greater feelings of closeness, physically and emotionally, and works as a buffer against the stresses of daily life.

Having to cope with issues surrounding work, money, and family can take a toll on the more enjoyable aspects of relationships. Experiencing play and engaging in shared hobbies offers a balance against the stress we incur during the week. If you and your partner already share many of these activities, that's wonderful! Keep enjoying them and find even more to do. If you don't, make the effort to find some activities you can both enjoy. Discuss your ideas, and experiment. The positive emotions this part of your life together brings forth will absolutely benefit your relationship for years to come.

Do you and your partner share a love for certain activities?

– 46 –

Couples who do everything together cannot survive

We have all seen those inseparable couples who do everything together. Everywhere they go, everything they do, one is almost never without the other. There may be many different reasons why a couple feels the need to be so tied together. Regardless of the reason, it is not a good idea to share too much. Such a relationship is codependent, and these couples have a fused identity. I've even come across couples who each answer the phone as "John-Mary" or "Mary-John," having gone so far as to combine their names.

The notion of sacrificing individual identity in order to find connection with a partner is a toxic one. These are the couples who either never argue or argue too much of the time, and these couples are stuck. They don't mature as individuals. Their relationships are characterized by a lack of trust and an infantilization of each other. They need each other too much. The two people who constitute a couple should always take their own space, have their own friends, do their own things, and have their own unshared areas of interest. This allows each individual to continue to grow as an adult and brings new, revitalizing energy to the partnership. Otherwise, it will become stagnant and will fail to progress.

The greatest relationships are those in which each individual finds balance by taking his own space and pursuing his own interests. These couples continue to enrich each other's lives by contributing to the creation of new, shared experiences. The act of separating and coming together becomes a delicate, refined dance, then, that brings the relationship an ever-expanding life. If you find that you don't have your own life's goals in place, look inward and start to figure out what you need for yourself. The time will be well spent, and the energy that you will attain will be nurturing for your relationship.

> *Do you think that you and your mate spend too much time together?*

– 47 –

Be careful not to control or to be controlled in your relationship

What do we all fear in an intimate relationship? I believe we all fear being left alone or abandoned by someone about whom we care deeply. Unfortunately, the intense pain accompanying this experience is something we have all probably had in our lifetime. The incredible hurt and sadness triggered by this event leaves an indelible imprint on our minds and our hearts. I have heard many times, "I was so hurt that I will never let it happen again!" Unfortunately, we don't have ultimate control of outcomes during the course of our lifetime with a spouse. This feeling of complete powerlessness is one of the main reasons the possibility of abandonment is so fear-inducing. Unfortunately, the only way we can completely avoid the possibility of abandonment is to never be vulnerable or open to another human being. To be truly safe from abandonment, we'd have to live in isolation without the possibility of love and intimacy. Luckily, most of us are not so emotionally scarred as to make this choice, but in choosing love, we must admit to ourselves that we are risking being left alone again.

Many of us will try to control the relationship in response to this fear. We may want to know everything our partner does when separated from us. We may question intensely our partner's relationship with other people. We may find we are micromanaging our partner's life. Ironically, behaving this way can lead to the realization of your worst fear. Your partner may react by distancing herself and keeping things to herself to avoid your controlling behaviors. You need to talk to your partner and allow her to see your vulnerability and your fears. If you have made a good choice, she will be understanding and respectful of where you're coming from. She may even share some of your insecurities. These conversations will end up giving you an increased sense of closeness and security.

The more emotional understanding you have of yourself and your partner, the more you instill a feeling of stability and faith in your relationship. Even though you can't ever prove that you will always be there for each other, you can learn to trust in each other's love. This is a deep sense of security, which is both attainable and real.

> *Are either of you trying to control the other out of fear of abandonment?*

− 48 −

Practice, practice, practice

We all know the joke: How do you get to Carnegie Hall? The punch line: Practice, practice, practice! This holds true for achieving a great relationship. Let me start by clarifying what I mean by practice. Take practicing the piano. Practice is not taking ten minutes to play scales the day before your lesson and then complaining to your teacher that you really don't "get it." I am familiar with this kind of work ethic because that was my approach to the piano until my mother pulled the plug on my lessons, insisting all the while, as parents do, that I'd regret it as a grown-up. Of course, she was right. For all my childhood and much of my adolescence, I had no idea what defined good practice. As an adult, I learned that it is defined by consistently engaging in some activity with heightened awareness toward a desired goal of improvement. If you are practicing piano, you will play scales with the goal of mastering your instrument. In swimming, you will work on your stroke, paying attention to any bad habits and focusing on the good ones to perfect your technique. It takes a lot of time and repetition to learn new patterns and build them into our brains.

In addition, we all have bad habits that need to be unlearned. Playing the piano may create tension in your arm, for example. Your goal becomes to unlearn what is creating the tension while learning to engage the right muscles efficiently. In a relationship, the goal is to become more fluid and productive in communicating so that we can bring about greater intimacy. You need to break bad communication habits and replace them with good ones. Many chapters of this book outline techniques that will improve your relationship with consistent practice.

The great thing about regular practice is that our bodies and brains are designed to integrate these new lessons. This means you don't need to be perfect in your execution while rehearsing. The process is always messy, so don't judge yourself or your partner. It is the commitment to finding consistency that is vital. If you keep up your commitment to practicing, despite the inevitable frustrations and setbacks, you will improve your relationship immeasurably.

> *Do you have the determination to consistently practice positive behaviors in the relationship to create a better life for you and your partner? Does your partner?*

– 49 –

Connect to your partner in a physical (but nonsexual) way every day

Touch is essential to sustaining intimate relationships. By touch, I mean kissing before leaving the house, putting a hand on her shoulder while talking, hugging her while she's cooking in the kitchen. You should look for as many opportunities as you can to physically express your affection in small ways during your time together throughout the day. Physical closeness of this kind fosters a very deep and growing sense of being loved, supported, and accepted. Establishing the habit of daily contact creates more and more positive regard within a couple. This is incredibly helpful given the inevitable miscommunications and stresses that can interrupt a given day.

Connecting physically provides a loving, subconscious

backdrop against which any unpleasant exchange can be ameliorated. In other words, each of these acts serves to inoculate us against the forces of stress and hurt between partners. I find that couples who consistently practice such interaction have a much greater level of respect, happiness, and fulfillment in their relationship. They also feel less frightened during times of stress and conflict. When life is stressful, a little voice inside keeps saying, It's all going to work out; remember how close you are and how much you express it to each other every day.

The effort required here is not enormous, but it does take awareness. Little gestures each day throughout your time together count. Remember to connect in the small ways, and you will be building a very positive foundation for the rest of your life.

Do you hug, touch, or kiss your partner every day?

– 50 –

Express frequent gratitude about what you like and love about your partner

It is very easy in a relationship to begin taking our partner and the relationship for granted. The days of unbridled rapture and newness are long gone. The incredible excitement of discovering new aspects of our partner feels like a faded memory. Life gets more complicated, responsibilities increase, and our attention is focused on many other things, unlike in the beginning, when the focus was mostly on each other. The act of remaining aware of what we appreciate about our partner is something that takes determination and resolve. We must realize that no matter how smoothly the relationship is running, it needs frequent nourishment. In this case, that source of energy and nourishment comes in the form of continuing to be appreciated and loved by our partner. Even after many, many years, nothing feels quite so good as an unexpected expression of love and gratitude from the one you have chosen to share your life with.

Furthermore, your heightened awareness on a daily basis of what you feel grateful for increases your feelings of attraction for and connection with your partner. This process reinforces itself. Couples who make the effort see exponential returns on their investment and improve every aspect of their relationship. Expressing gratitude and outwardly delighting in your partner is the greatest gift you can give yourself and one of the greatest things you can do for your relationship. Don't wait. Start noticing now, and you will see the benefits immediately.

Do you frequently share what you appreciate about your partner?

– 51 –

The Golden Rule

Treat your lover as you would like to be treated. This principle is so simple to understand but so difficult to uphold. However, committing to this practice daily is the easiest way to make sure you stay on the right path. Read a chapter or two of this book each day. Take it out at lunch, on the bus, and read it at home before bed. As you digest the techniques and tools in this book, these 51 things will become intuitive. This means that during your interactions with your partner, you will be reminded of them and be able to apply them in your relationship. You will find yourself responding more and more clearly to previously confusing situations. In time, you will make them your own and your confidence will show. You will communicate with fluidity and empathy while making sure your needs are being met on a consistent basis. You will know that your choices are grounded and based on evidence, not on impulse. When you choose to get engaged, you will trust that choice with all your being, and your wedding day will be a beautiful confirmation of that choice. My wish is for your path always to be clear and bright, filled with love and true intimacy for the rest of your days. Good luck!

Do you treat your lover as you wish to be treated?

Notes